STRAIGHTFORWARD THOUGHTS FOR YOUNG MEN

Register This New Book

Benefits of Registering*

- ✓ FREE **replacements** of lost or damaged books
- ✓ FREE **audiobook** – *Pilgrim's Progress*, audiobook edition
- ✓ FREE information about new titles and other **freebies**

www.anekopress.com/new-book-registration

*See our website for requirements and limitations.

STRAIGHTFORWARD THOUGHTS FOR YOUNG MEN

What Every Young Man
Must Consider Now,
Before It's Too Late

J. C. Ryle

We love hearing from our readers. Please contact us at www.anekopress.com/questions-comments with any questions, comments, or suggestions.

Straightforward Thoughts for Young Men – J. C. Ryle
Revised Edition Copyright © 2019
First edition published 1886

All rights reserved. No part of this book may be reproduced, stored in a retrieval system, or transmitted in any form or by any means – electronic, mechanical, photocopying, recording, or otherwise, without written permission from the publisher.

Scripture quotations are taken from the Jubilee Bible, copyright © 2000, 2001, 2010, 2013 by Russell M. Stendal. Used by permission of Russell M. Stendal, Bogota, Colombia. All rights reserved.

Cover Design: J. Martin
Cover Images: By vectortatu/Shutterstock
Editors: Ruth Clark

Printed in the United States of America
Aneko Press
www.anekopress.com
Aneko Press, Life Sentence Publishing, and our logos are trademarks of
Life Sentence Publishing, Inc.
203 E. Birch Street
P.O. Box 652
Abbotsford, WI 54405

RELIGION / Christian Living / Spiritual Growth

Paperback ISBN: 978-1-62245-621-5
eBook ISBN: 978-1-62245-622-2

10 9 8 7 6 5 4 3 2 1

Available where books are sold

Contents

Introduction ix

Ch. 1: Why I'm Writing to Young Men 1

Ch. 2: Real Dangers to Young Men 19

Ch. 3: Some General Advice for Young Men 39

Ch. 4: Special Rules of Conduct for Young Men 59

Ch. 5: Conclusion 79

J. C. Ryle – A Brief Biography 85

Other Similar Titles 91

Introduction

When the apostle Paul wrote his epistle to Titus about his responsibility as a minister, he mentioned young men as a group requiring particular attention. After speaking of older men and older women, and young women, he adds this advice: *Young men likewise exhort to be temperate* (Titus 2:6). I am going to follow the apostle's advice. I propose to offer a few words of friendly exhortation to young men.

I am growing old myself, but there are few things that I can remember so well as the days of my youth. I have a most distinct recollection of the joys and the sorrows, the hopes and the fears, the temptations and the difficulties, the mistaken judgments and the misplaced affections, and the errors and the aspirations which surround and accompany a young man's life. If I can only say something to keep some young man walking in the right way and preserve him from faults and sins, which may hurt his prospects both for time and eternity, I shall be very thankful. There are four things which I propose to do:

1. I will mention some general *reasons* why young men need exhorting.

2. I will note some special *dangers* which young men need to be warned about.

3. I will give some general *advice* which I beg young men to receive.

4. I will set down some special *rules of conduct* which I strongly advise young men to follow.

On each of these four points I have something to say, and I pray to God that what I say may do good to some soul.

1

Why I'm Writing to Young Men

What are the general reasons why young men need specific exhortation? I will mention several of them in order.

(1) For one thing, there is the painful fact that there are few young men anywhere who seem to be Christians.

I speak without respect of persons; I say it of all. Rich or poor, gentle or rough, educated or uneducated, in the city or in the country – it makes no difference. I shudder to think how few young men are led by the Spirit, how few are on that narrow road which leads to life, how few are setting their affections on things above, how few are taking up the cross and following Christ. I say all this with sorrow, but I believe, in God's sight, that I am saying nothing more than the truth.

Young men, you form a large and very important class in the population of this country; but where, and in what condition, are your souls? Regardless of where we turn for an answer, the report will be one and the same! Let us ask any faithful minister of the gospel and note what he tells us. How many unmarried young people can he remember who come to the Lord's Supper? Who are the most backward about the doctrines of salvation, the most irregular about Sunday services, the most difficult to draw to weekly Bible studies and prayer meetings, the most inattentive to whatever is being preached? Which part of his congregation fills him with the most anxiety? Who are the Reubens for whom he has the deepest *searchings of the heart* (Judges 5:16)? Who in his flock are the hardest to manage, who require the most frequent warnings and rebukes, who cause him the greatest uneasiness and sorrow, who keep him most constantly in fear for their souls, and who seem the most hopeless? Depend on it, his answer will always be, "The young men!"

Let us ask the parents in any county throughout this land, and see what they will generally say. Who in their families give them the most pain and trouble? Who need the most watchfulness, and who most often provoke and disappoint them? Who are the first to be led away from what is right, and the last to remember cautions and good advice? Who are the most difficult to keep in order and limits? Who most frequently break out into open sin, disgrace the name they bear, make their friends unhappy, embitter the older relatives, and cause them to die with sorrow in their hearts? Depend on it, the answer will generally be, "The young men!"

Let us ask the judges and police officers and note what they reply. Who goes to the nightclubs and bars the most? Who make up street gangs? Who are most often arrested for drunkenness, disturbing the peace, fighting, stealing, assaults, and the like? Who fill the jails and penitentiaries and detention homes? Who are the class which requires the most incessant watching and looking after? Depend on it, they will at once point to the same group and they will say, "The young men!"

Let us turn to the upper classes and note the report we get from them. In one family, the sons are always wasting time, health, and money in the selfish pursuit of pleasure. In another, the sons will follow no profession and will fritter away the most precious years of their life in doing nothing. In another, they take up a profession as a mere form, but pay no attention to its duties. In another, they are always forming wrong connections, gambling, getting into debt, associating with bad companions, and keeping their friends in a constant fever of anxiety. Note that rank, title, wealth, and education do not prevent these things! Anxious fathers, heartbroken mothers, and sorrowing sisters could tell sad stories about them, if the truth were known. Many a family, with everything this world can give, numbers among its relatives some name that is never named, or only named with regret and shame; some son, some brother, some cousin, or some nephew who will have his own way and is a grief to all who know him.

There is seldom a rich family that hasn't got some thorn in its side, some blot on its page of happiness, or some constant source of pain and anxiety; and often, far too often, the true cause is, "The young men!"

What shall we say to these things? These are facts, plain facts, facts which meet us on every side, facts which cannot be denied. How dreadful this is! How dreadful the thought that every time I meet a young man, I meet one who is in all probability an enemy of God, traveling on the wide road which leads to hell, unfit for heaven! Surely, with such facts before me, will you not wonder why I exhort you? You must allow that there is a good reason.

> **Young men, it is appointed for you to die.**

(2) Death and judgment are waiting for young men, even as they wait for others, and they nearly all seem to forget it.

Young men, it is appointed for you to die, and no matter how strong and healthy you may be now, the day of your death is perhaps very near. I see young people sick as well as the elderly. I bury youthful corpses as well as aged. I read the names of persons no older than yourselves in every graveyard. I learn from books that except for infancy and old age, more die between thirteen and twenty-three than at any other period of life. And yet you live as if you were sure that presently you will never die.

Are you thinking you will pay attention to these things tomorrow? Remember the words of Solomon: *Boast not thyself of tomorrow for thou knowest not what a day may bring forth* (Proverbs 27:1). "I will worry about serious things tomorrow," said an unsaved person to one who warned him of coming danger; but his tomorrow never came. Tomorrow is the devil's day, but today is God's. Satan does not care how spiritual your intentions are, or how holy your resolutions, if only they are determined to be done tomorrow. Oh, give no place to the devil in this matter! All men don't live to be elderly fathers like Isaac and Jacob. Many children die before their fathers. David had to mourn the death of his two finest sons; Job lost all of his ten children in one day. Your lot may be like one of theirs, and when death comes, it will be vain to talk of tomorrow; you must go at once.

Do you think that you will have a more convenient time to think about these things? So thought Felix and the Athenians to whom Paul preached, but it never came. The road to hell is paved with such ideas. Better make sure to work while you can. Leave nothing unsettled that is eternal. Run no risk when your soul is at stake. Believe me, the salvation of a soul is no easy matter. Everyone needs a *great salvation*, whether young or old; all need to be born again – all need to be washed in Christ's blood – all need to be sanctified by the Spirit. Happy is that man who does not leave these things uncertain, but never rests until he has the witness of the Spirit within him, testifying to him that he is a child of God.

Young men, your time is short. Your days are but a brief shadow, a mist that appears for a little while and then vanishes, a story that is soon told. Your bodies are not made of brass. *The young men faint and are weary; the children stumble and fall*, says Isaiah (Isaiah 40:30). Your health may be taken from you in a moment: it only needs an accident, a fever, an inflammation, or a broken blood vessel, and the worm will soon feed upon you in the grave. There is but a step between any one of you and death. This night your soul might be required of you. You are fast going the way of all the earth; you will soon be gone. Your life is all uncertainty, your death and judgment are perfectly sure. You too must hear the archangel's trumpet and go forth to stand before the great white throne of judgment; you too must obey that summons which Jerome says was always ringing in his ears: "Get up, you dead, and come to judgment." *I come quickly* is the language of the judge Himself. I cannot, dare not, will not let you alone.

Oh, that you would all take to heart the words of the preacher: *Rejoice, O young man, in thy youth; and let thy heart cheer thee in the days of thy youth and walk in the ways of thine heart and in the sight of thine eyes; but know thou, that for all these things God will bring thee into judgment* (Ecclesiastes 11:9). Amazing, that with such a prospect of coming judgment, any man can be careless and unconcerned! Surely, none are so crazy as those who are content to live unprepared to die. Surely, the unbelief of men is the most amazing thing in the world. The clearest prophecy in the Bible begins with these words: *Who shall believe our report?* (Isaiah 53:1). The Lord Jesus said, *When the Son of Man comes, shall he find faith on the earth?* (Luke 18:8). Young men, I fear this will be the report of many of you in the courts above: "They will not believe." I fear you will be hurried out of the world and will awake to find out too late that death and judgment are realities. I fear all this, and therefore I exhort you.

(3) What young men will be in all probability depends on what they are now, and they seem to forget this.

Youth is the planting time of full age, the molding

season in the little space of human life, the turning point in the history of man's mind.

By the shoot that springs up we can judge the type of tree that is growing, by the blossoms we judge the kind of fruit, by the spring we judge the type of harvest coming, by the morning we judge the coming day, and by the character of the young man, we may generally judge what he will be when he grows up.

Young men, do not be deceived. Don't think you can, at will, serve lusts and pleasures in your beginning and then go and serve God with ease at your latter end. Don't think that you can live with Esau and then die with Jacob. It is a mockery to deal with God and your souls in such a fashion. It is an awful mockery to suppose you can give the flower of your strength to the world and the devil, and then put off the King of Kings with the scraps and remains of your heart, and the wreck and remnant of your power. It is an awful mockery, and you may find to your loss that the thing cannot be done.

I dare say you are planning on a late repentance. You do not know what you are doing. You are planning without God. Repentance and faith are the gifts of

God, and they are gifts that He often withholds, when they have been long offered in vain. I grant you, true repentance is never too late, but I warn you at the same time that late repentance is seldom true. I grant you, one penitent thief was converted in his last hours, so that no man might despair. But I warn you, only one was converted, so that no man might presume. I grant you, it is written, Jesus is *able also to save to the uttermost those that come unto God by him* (Hebrews 7:25). But I warn you, it is also written by the same Spirit, *Because I have called and ye refused; I have stretched out my hand, and no one responded; I also will laugh at your calamity; I will mock when your fear comes upon you* (Proverbs 1:24, 26).

Believe me, you will find it no easy matter to turn to God whenever you please. It is a true saying of the godly Leighton: "The way of sin is downhill; a man cannot stop when he wants to." Holy desires and serious convictions are not like the servants of the centurion, ready to come and go at your desire; rather, they are like the unicorn in Job: they will not obey your voice, nor attend to your bidding. It was said of the famous general Hannibal of old, that when he could have taken the city he warred against, he would not, and in time when he would have, he could not. Beware lest the same kind of thing happens to you in the matter of eternal life.

Why do I say all this? I say it because of the force of habit. I say it because experience tells me that people's hearts are seldom changed if they are not changed when young. Seldom indeed are men converted when they are old. Habits have deep roots. Once sin is allowed to settle in your heart, it will not be turned out at your bidding. Custom becomes second nature, and its chains are not easily broken. The prophet has well said, *Can the Ethiopian change his skin or the leopard his spots? Likewise ye also cannot do good, being taught to do evil* (Jeremiah 13:23). Habits are like stones rolling downhill – the farther they roll, the faster and more ungovernable is their course. Habits, like trees, are strengthened by age. A boy may bend an oak when it is a sapling, but a hundred men cannot root it up when it is a full-grown tree. A child can wade over the Thames River at its fountainhead, and the largest ship in the world can float in it when it gets near the sea. So it is with habits: the older, the stronger – the longer they have held possession, the harder they will be to cast out. They grow with our growth, and strengthen with our strength. Custom is the nurse of sin. Every fresh act of sin lessens fear and remorse, hardens our hearts, blunts the edge of our conscience, and increases our evil inclination.

Young men, you may fancy I am laying too much stress on this point. If you had seen old men, as I have, on the brink of the grave, without any feelings, seared, callous, dead, cold, and hard as stone – you would not think so. Believe me, you cannot stand still in your souls. Habits of good or evil are daily strengthening in your hearts. Every day you are either getting nearer to God, or further off. Every year that you continue to be unrepentant, the wall of division between you and heaven becomes higher and thicker, and the gulf to be crossed deeper and broader. Oh, dread the hardening effect of constant lingering in sin! Now is the accepted time. See that your decision not be put off until the winter of your days. If you do not seek the Lord when young, the strength of habit is such that you will probably never seek Him at all.

> Every day you are either getting nearer to God, or further off.

I fear this, and therefore I exhort you.

(4) The devil uses special diligence to destroy the souls of young men, and they don't seem to know it.

Satan knows very well that you will make up the next generation, and therefore, he employs every trick to make you his own. I would not have you be ignorant of his schemes.

You are those on whom he puts his choicest temptations. He spreads his net with the most watchful carefulness to entangle your hearts. He baits his trap with the sweetest morsels to get you into his power. He displays his wares before your eyes with his utmost ingenuity in order to make you buy his sugared poisons and eat his accursed treats. You are the grand object of his attack. May the Lord rebuke him and deliver you out of his hands.

Young men, beware of being taken by his snares. He will try to throw dust in your eyes and prevent you from seeing anything in its true colors. He would eagerly make you think that evil is good and good is evil. He will paint, cover with gold, and dress up sin in order to make you fall in love with it. He will deform, misrepresent, and fabricate true Christianity in order to make you take a dislike to it. He will exalt the pleasures of wickedness – but he will hide from you the sting. He will lift up before your eyes the cross and its painfulness – but he will keep out of sight the eternal crown. He will promise you everything, as he did to Christ, if you will only serve him. He will even help you to wear a form of Christianity, if you will only neglect the power. He will tell you at the beginning of your lives that it is too soon to serve God – he will tell you at the end that it is too late. Oh, do not be deceived!

You don't know the danger you are in from this Enemy; and it is this very ignorance which makes me afraid. You are like blind men, walking among holes and pitfalls; you do not see the perils which are around you on every side.

Your Enemy is mighty. He is called *the prince of this world* (John 14:30). He opposed our Lord Jesus Christ all through His ministry. He tempted Adam and Eve to eat the forbidden fruit and so brought sin and death into the world. He even tempted David, the man after God's own heart, and caused his latter days to be full of sorrow. He even tempted Peter, the chosen apostle, and made him deny his Lord. Surely, his hostility towards man and God is to be despised.

Your Enemy is restless. He never sleeps. He is always going around like a roaring lion, seeking whom he may devour. He is always going back and forth in the earth and walking up and down on it. You may be careless about your souls, but he is not. He wants your soul to make you miserable, like himself, and he will have your soul if he can. Surely, his hatred towards men and God is to be despised.

And your Enemy is cunning. For thousands of years he has been reading one book, and that book is the heart of man. He ought to know it well, and he does know it – all its weakness, all its deceitfulness, all its folly. And he has a storehouse full of temptations, such as are most likely to do the heart of man the most harm. Never will you go to the place where he will not find you. Go into the city – he will be there. Go into the wilderness – he will be there also. Sit among drunkards – and he will be there to help you. Listen to preaching – and he will be there to distract you. Surely, such ill will is to be despised.

Young men, this Enemy is working hard for your destruction, however little you may think it. You are the prize which he is specially contending for. He foresees you must either be the blessings or the curses of your day, and he is trying hard to effect a place in your hearts early in your life in order that you may help advance his kingdom each day. Well does he understand that to spoil the bud is the surest way to mar the flower.

Oh, that your eyes were opened, like those of Elisha's servant! Oh, that you could see what Satan is scheming against your peace! I must warn you – I must exhort you. Whether you will hear or not, I cannot, dare not, leave you alone.

(5) Young men need exhorting because of the sorrow it will save them to begin serving God now.

Sin is the mother of all sorrow, and no sort of sin appears to give a man so much misery and pain as the sins of his youth. The foolish acts he did, the time he wasted, the mistakes he made, the bad company he kept, the harm he did himself in both body and soul, the chances of happiness he threw away, the openings of usefulness he neglected – all these things that often embitter the conscience of an old man throw a gloom on the evening of his days, and fill later hours of his life with self-reproach and shame.

Some men could tell you of the untimely loss of health brought on by youthful sins. Disease racks their limbs with pain, and life is almost a weariness. Their muscular strength is so wasted that the slightest weight seems a burden. Their eyes have become prematurely dim and their natural energy abated. The sun of their health has gone down while it is yet day, and they mourn to see their flesh and body consumed. Believe me, this is a bitter cup to drink.

Others could give you sad accounts of the consequences of idleness. They threw away the golden opportunity for learning. They would not get wisdom at the time when their minds were most able to receive it and their memory most ready to retain it. And now

> Lost time can never be redeemed.

it is too late. They don't have the time to sit down and learn. They no longer have the same power, even if they had the time. Lost time can never be redeemed. This too is a bitter cup to drink.

Others could tell you of grievous mistakes in judgment from which they suffer all their lives. They had to have it their own way. They would not take advice. They formed some connection which has altogether ruined their happiness. They chose a profession for which they were entirely unsuited. And they see it all now. But their eyes are only open when the mistake cannot be retrieved. Oh, this is also a bitter cup to drink!

Young men, young men, I wish you knew the comfort of a conscience not burdened with a long list of youthful sins. These are the wounds that pierce the deepest. These are the arrows that drink up a man's spirit. This is the iron that enters into the soul. Be merciful to yourselves. Seek the Lord early, and you will be spared many a bitter tear.

This is the truth that Job seems to have felt. He says, *Why dost thou write bitter things against me and make me carry the iniquities of my youth* (Job 13:26). So also his friend Zophar, speaking of the wicked, says, *His bones are full of the sins of his youth, which shall be buried with him in the dust* (Job 20:11).

David also seems to have felt it. He says to the Lord, *Remember not the sins of my youth, nor my rebellions* (Psalm 25:7).

Theodore Beza, the great Swiss Reformer, felt it so strongly that he named it in his will as a special mercy that he had been called out from the world, by the grace of God, at the age of sixteen.

Go and ask believers now, and I think many will tell you much the same. "Oh, that I could live my young days over again!" They will most probably say, "Oh, that

I had spent the beginning of my life in a better way! Oh, that I had not laid the foundation of evil habits so strongly in the springtime of my journey!"

Young men, I want to save you all this sorrow if I can. Hell itself is truth known too late. Be wise in time. What youth sows, old age must reap. Do not give the most precious season of your life to that which will not comfort you in the latter days of your life. Sow to yourselves rather in righteousness: break up your hard ground and don't sow among thorns.

Sin may be easy for you to do with your hands, or run smoothly off your tongue now, but depend on it, the effects of your sin and you will meet again in time, however little you might like it. Old wounds will often ache and give pain long after they are healed, and only a scar remains; so may you find it with your sins. The footprints of animals have been found on the surface of rocks that were once wet sand, thousands of years after the animals that made them have perished and passed away; so also is it with your sins.

> What youth sows, old age must reap.

"Experience," says the proverb, "is a hard school to attend, but fools will learn in no other." I want you all to escape the misery of learning in that school. I want you to avoid the wretchedness that youthful sins are sure to entail. This is the last reason why I exhort you.

2

Real Dangers to Young Men

There are some special dangers that young men need to be warned about.

(1) One danger to young men is pride.

I know well that all souls are in fearful peril. Old or young, it doesn't matter; all have a race to run, a battle to fight, a heart to humble, a world to overcome, a body to keep under control, and a devil to resist; and we may very well say, who is sufficient for these things? But still every age and condition has its own peculiar snares and temptations, and it is well to know them. He that is forewarned is forearmed. If I can only persuade you to be on your guard against the dangers I am going to name, I am sure I shall do your souls an essential service.

Pride is the oldest sin in the world. Indeed, it was

before the world. Satan and his angels fell by pride. They were not satisfied with their first situation and status. Thus, pride stocked hell with its first inhabitants.

Pride threw Adam out of Paradise. He was not content with the place God assigned him. He tried to raise himself, and he fell. Thus, sin, sorrow, and death entered in by pride.

Pride sits in all our hearts by nature. We are born proud. Pride makes us rest content with ourselves, makes us think we are good enough as we are, keeps us from taking advice, makes us refuse the gospel of Christ, and turns everyone to his own way. But pride never reigns anywhere so powerfully as in the heart of a young man.

How common it is to see young men with big heads and who are high-minded and impatient with any counsel! How often they are rude and uncourteous to all around them, thinking they are not valued and honored as they deserve! How often will they not stop to listen to a hint from an older person! They think that they know everything. They are full of conceit of their own wisdom. They think elderly people, and especially their relatives, are stupid, dull, and slow. They want no teaching or instruction themselves: they understand all things. It almost makes them angry to be spoken to. Like young horses, they cannot bear the least control. They must be independent and have their own way.

They seem to think, like those whom Job mentioned, *No doubt but ye are the people, and wisdom shall die with you* (Job 12:2). And all this is pride.

Rehoboam was such a person, who despised the counsel of the old, experienced men who stood before his father, and listened to the advice of the young men of his own generation. He lived to reap the consequences of his folly. There are many like him.

The prodigal son in the parable was also such a person, who needed to have his share of the inheritance so he could set himself up in the lifestyle that he desired. He could not submit to living quietly under his father's roof, but wanted to go into a far country and be his own master. Like the little child that will leave its mother's hand and walk alone, he soon feels the sting of his folly. He became wiser when he had to eat husks with the swine. But there are many like him.

Beware of pride.

Young men, I beseech you earnestly, beware of pride. Two things are said to be very rare sights in the world – one is a young man who is humble, and the other is an old man who is content. I fear that this is only too true.

Do not be proud of your own abilities, your own strength, your own knowledge, your own appearance, or your own cleverness. Do not be proud of yourself and your endowments of any kind. It all comes from not knowing yourself and the world. The older you grow, and the more you see, the less reason you will find for being proud. Ignorance and inexperience are the pedestal of pride; once the pedestal is removed, pride will soon come down.

Remember how often Scripture sets before us the excellence of a humble spirit. How strongly we are warned *not to obtain more knowledge than is prudent to know* (Romans 12:3). How plainly we are told, *If anyone thinks that they know anything, they know nothing yet as they ought to know* (1 Corinthians 8:2). How strict is the command to be *clothed, . . . with bowels of . . . humility* (Colossians 3:12). And again, *Be clothed with humility* (1 Peter 5:5). This is the garment of which many seem not to have so much as a rag.

Think of the great example our Lord Jesus Christ leaves us in this respect. He washed the feet of His disciples, saying, *For I have given you an example that ye should do as I have done to you* (John 13:15). It is written, *Though he was rich, yet for your sakes he became poor* (2 Corinthians 8:9). And again, *[He] emptied himself, taking the form of a slave, made in the likeness of men, and being found in fashion as a man, he humbled himself* (Philippians 2:7-8). Surely, to be proud is to be more like the devil and fallen Adam than like Christ.

Think of the wisest man that ever lived – I mean

Solomon. See how he speaks of himself as a *tender young man*, as one who does not *know how to go out or come in* (1 Kings 3:7). That was a very different spirit from his brother Absalom, who thought himself equal to anything: *Oh, that I were made judge in the land, that everyone who has any suit or cause might come unto me, and I would do him justice!* (2 Samuel 15:4). That was a very different spirit from his brother Adonijah, *who exalted himself, saying, I will reign* (1 Kings 1:5). Humility was the beginning of Solomon's wisdom. He writes it down as his own experience: *Seest thou a man wise in his own conceit? there is more hope of a fool than of him* (Proverbs 26:12).

Young men, take to heart the Scriptures just quoted. Do not be too confident in your own judgment. Stop being so sure that you are always right and others are wrong. Don't trust your own opinion when you find it contrary to that of older men, and especially when you find it contrary to that of your own parents. Age gives experience and therefore deserves respect. It is a mark of Elihu's wisdom in the book of Job, that *Elihu had waited until Job had spoken because they were all elder than he* (Job 32:4). And afterwards, he said, *I am younger, and ye are older; therefore, I was afraid, and I feared to declare unto you my opinion. I said, Days shall speak, and the multitude of years shall declare wisdom* (Job 32:6-7). Humility and silence are beautiful graces in young people. Never be ashamed of being a learner: Jesus was one at twelve years old. When He was found in the temple, He was *sitting in the midst of the doctors, both hearing them and asking them questions* (Luke 2:46). The wisest men would tell you they are always learners and are humbled to find out after all how little they know. The great Sir Isaac Newton used to say that he felt himself no better than a little child who had picked up a few precious stones on the shore of the sea of knowledge.

Young men, if you would be wise, if you would be happy, remember the warning I give you – beware of pride.

(2) Another danger to young men is the love of pleasure.

Youth is the time when our passions are strongest and, like unruly children, we cry most loudly for indulgence. Youth is the time when we generally have our most health and strength; death seems far away, and to enjoy ourselves in this life seems to be everything. Youth is the time when most people have few earthly cares or anxieties to take up their attention. And all these things help to make young men think of nothing except pleasure. "I serve lusts and pleasures": that is the true answer many a young man would give if asked, "Whose servant are you?"

Young men, time would not permit me to tell you

all the fruits this love of pleasure produces, and all the ways in which it may do you harm. Why should I speak of carousing, partying, drinking, gambling, movie-going, dancing, and the like? There are few to be found who don't know something of these things by bitter experience. And these are only instances. All things that give a feeling of excitement for the time, all things that drown thought and keep the mind in a constant whirl, all things that please the senses and delight the flesh – these are the sorts of things that have mighty power at your time of life, and they owe their power to the love of pleasure. Be on your guard. Do not be like those of whom Paul speaks as *lovers of pleasure more than lovers of God* (2 Timothy 3:4).

> Remember what I say: if you would cling to earthly pleasures, these are the things that murder souls.

Remember what I say: if you would cling to earthly pleasures, these are the things that murder souls. There is no surer way to get a seared conscience and a hard heart towards the things of God than to give way to the desires of the flesh and mind. It seems like nothing at first, but it tells in the long run.

Consider what Peter says: *Abstain from the carnal desires which war against the soul* (1 Peter 2:11). They destroy the soul's peace, break down its strength, lead it into captivity, and make it a slave.

Consider what Paul says: *Mortify therefore your members which are upon the earth: fornication, uncleanness, inordinate affection, evil lust, and covetousness, which is idolatry* (Colossians 3:5). *For those that are of the Christ have crucified the flesh with its affections and lusts* (Galatians 5:24). Once the body was a perfect home for a soul, and now it is all corrupt and disordered and needs constant watching. It is a burden to the soul – not a helper; it is a hindrance – not an assistance. It may become a useful servant, but it is always a bad master.

Consider again the words of Paul: *But be clothed with the Lord Jesus Christ, and do not listen to the flesh, to fulfil its desires* (Romans 13:14). "These," says Leighton, "are the words, the very reading of which gave Augustine a great conviction of heart, causing an immoral young man to be turned into a faithful servant of Jesus Christ." Young men, I wish this might be the case with all of you.

Remember again that if you cling to earthly pleasures, they will all be unsatisfying, empty, and pointless. Like the locusts of the vision in Revelation, they seem to have crowns on their heads, but like the same locusts, you will find they have stings – real stings – in their tails. All that glitters is not gold. All that tastes sweet is not good. All that pleases for a while is not real pleasure.

Go and take your fill of earthly pleasures if you will; you will never find your heart satisfied with them.

There will always be a voice within, crying like the leech in Proverbs 30:15, *Give, give.* There is an empty place there, which nothing but God can fill. You will find, as Solomon did by experience, that earthly pleasures are but a meaningless show – promising contentment but bringing a dissatisfaction of spirit; gold-plated caskets, exquisite to look at on the outside, but full of ashes and corruption within. Be wise in your youth. Write the word *poison* on all earthly pleasures. The most lawful of them must be used in moderation. All of them are soul destroying if you give them your heart. Pleasure must first have the guarantee that it is not sinful; then it is to be enjoyed in moderation.

And I will not shrink from warning all young men to remember the seventh commandment, to beware of adultery and sexual immorality and of all impurity of every kind. I fear that we don't very often speak on this part of God's law. But when I see how the prophets and the apostles have dealt with this subject, when I observe the open way in which the Reformers of our own church denounced it, when I see the number of young men who walk in the wicked footsteps of Reuben, Hophni, Phinehas, and Amnon, I for one cannot with a good conscience hold my peace. The world becomes more wicked because of our failure to teach and preach on this commandment. For my own part, I feel it would be false and unscriptural delicacy, in addressing men, not to speak of that which is preeminently the "young man's sin."

The violation of the seventh commandment is the sin above all others that, as Hosea says, *take[s] away the heart* (Hosea 4:11). It is the sin that leaves deeper scars upon the soul than any other sin that a man can commit. It is a sin that destroys thousands of young men in every age, and has even overthrown a few of the saints of God in the past. King David is fearful proof. It is the sin that man dares to smile at and smooths over using the terms *thrills, love, uncontrollable passions,* and *natural desires.* But it is the sin that the devil rejoices over, for he is the *unclean spirit*; and it is the sin that God abhors and declares He *will judge* (Hebrews 13:4).

Young men, *flee fornication* (1 Corinthians 6:18) if you love life. *Let no one deceive you with vain words, for because of these things the wrath of God comes upon the sons of disobedience* (Ephesians 5:6). Flee from the opportunity of it, from the company of those who might draw you into it, and from the places where you might be tempted to do it. Read what our Lord says about it in Matthew 5:28: *I say unto you, That whosoever who looks on a woman to lust after her has committed adultery with her already in his heart.* Be like the holy servant Job: *I made a covenant with my eyes; why then should I look upon a maid?* (Job 31:1). Flee from talking about it. It is one of the things that ought not even be hinted at in conversation. You cannot even touch black grease without getting your hands dirty. Flee from the thoughts of it; resist them, destroy them, pray much; make any sacrifice rather than give way to them. Imagination is the hotbed where this sin is too often hatched. Guard your thoughts, and there will be little fear about your actions.

Consider the caution I have been giving. If you forget everything else, do not let this be forgotten.

(3) Another danger to young men is thoughtlessness.

Not thinking is one simple reason why thousands of souls are thrown away forever into the lake of fire. Men will not consider, will not look ahead, will not look around them, and will not reflect on the end of their present course and the sure consequences of their present days, and will wake up to find they are damned for a lack of thinking.

> Guard your thoughts, and there will be little fear about your actions.

Young men, none are in more danger of this than yourselves. You know little of the perils around you, and so you are careless about how you walk. You hate the trouble of serious, quiet thinking, and so you make wrong decisions and bring upon yourselves much sorrow. Young Esau had to have his brother's stew and sold his birthright; he never thought how much he would want it in the future. Young Simeon and Levi had to avenge the rape of their sister Dinah and kill the Shechemites; they never considered how much trouble and anxiety they might bring on their father, Jacob, and his house. Job seems to have been especially afraid of this thoughtlessness among his children. It is written, that when they had a feast, and *when the days of their banquets were over, that Job sent and sanctified them and rose up early in the morning and offered burnt offerings according to the number for them all; for Job said, It may be that my sons have sinned and blasphemed God in their hearts. Thus did Job continually* (Job 1:5).

Believe me, this world is not a world in which we can do well without thinking, and least of all do well in the matter of our souls. "Don't think," whispers Satan, for he knows that an unconverted heart is like a dishonest businessman's financial records – they will not bear close inspection. *Consider your ways*, says the Word of God – stop and think, consider and be wise. The Spanish proverb says it well: "Hurry comes from the devil." Just as men marry in a rush and then are miserable with their mate, so they make mistakes about their souls in a minute and then suffer for it for years. Just as a bad servant does wrong and then says, "I never gave it a thought," so young men run into sin and then say, "I did not think about it – it did not look like sin." Not look like sin! What would you expect? Sin will not come to you, saying, "I am sin"; it would do little harm if it did. Sin always seems good and pleasant and desirable at the time of commission. Oh, get wisdom, get discretion! Remember the words of Solomon: *Ponder the path of thy feet, and let all thy ways be established* (Proverbs 4:26).

Some, I dare say, will object that I am asking what is unreasonable; that youth is not the time of life when people ought to be grave and thoughtful. I answer, there is little likelihood of their being too much so in the present day. Foolish talking and kidding, joking, and excessive amusement are only too common. I don't argue the fact that there is a time for all things, but to be always flippant and joking is anything but wise. What does the wisest of men say? *It is better to go to the house of mourning than to go to the house of feasting, for that is the end of all men; and the living will lay it to his heart. Sorrow is better than laughter; for by the sadness of the countenance the heart is made whole. The heart of the wise is in the house of mourning, but the heart of fools is in the house of pleasure* (Ecclesiastes 7:2-4). Matthew Henry tells a story of a great statesman in Queen Elizabeth's time who retired from public life in his latter days and gave himself up to serious thought. His former merry companions came to visit him and told him that he was becoming somber. "No," he replied, "I am serious; for everyone around me is serious. God is serious in observing us; Christ is serious in interceding for us; the Spirit is serious in striving with us; the truths of God are serious; our spiritual enemies are serious in their endeavors to ruin us; and poor lost sinners are serious in hell. Why then should you and I not be serious too?"

Oh, young men, learn to be thoughtful! Learn to consider what you are doing and where you are going. Make time for calm reflection. Commune with your own heart and be still. Remember my caution – do not be lost merely for the lack of thought.

(4) Another danger to young men is contempt of Christianity.

This also is one of your special dangers. I always observe that none pay so little outward respect to Christianity as young men. None take so little part in our services when they are present at them, or use Bibles so little, or sing so little, or listen to preaching so little. None are so generally absent at prayer meetings, Bible studies, and all other weekday helps to the soul. Young men seem to think they do not need these things – they may be good for women and old men, but not for them. They appear ashamed of seeming to care about their souls; one would almost fancy they considered it a disgrace to go to heaven at all. And this is contempt of Christianity – it is the same spirit which made the young people of Bethel mock Elisha; and of this spirit I say to all young men, beware! If it is worthwhile to be a Christian, it is worthwhile to be in earnest about it.

Contempt of holy things is the straight road to hell. Once a man begins to make a joke of any part of Christianity, then I am never surprised to hear that he has turned out to be an unbeliever.

Young men, have you really made up your minds to this? Have you clearly looked into the fires which are before you, if you persist in despising Christianity? Call to mind the words of David: *The fool has said in his heart, There is no God* (Psalm 14:1). The fool, and no one but the fool, has said it, but he has never proved it! Remember, if there ever was a book which has been proved true from beginning to end, by every kind of evidence, that book is the Bible. It has defied the attacks of all enemies and faultfinders. *The word of the LORD is precise* (Psalm 18:30). It has been tested in every way, and the more it has been tested, the more evidently has it been shown to be the very handiwork of God Himself. What will you believe if you do not believe the Bible? There is no choice but to believe something ridiculous and absurd. Depend on it, no man is so grossly naive as the man

> If it is worthwhile to be a Christian, it is worthwhile to be in earnest about it.

who denies the Bible to be the Word of God; and as it is the Word of God, be careful that you don't despise it.

Men may tell you that there are difficulties in the Bible, things hard to understand. It would not be God's book if there were not. And what if there are? You don't despise medicines because you cannot explain all that your doctor does with them. But whatever men may say, the things needed for salvation are as clear as daylight. Be very sure of this – people never reject the Bible because they cannot understand it. They understand it too well; they understand that it condemns their own behavior; they understand that it witnesses against their own sins and summons them to judgment. They try to believe it is false and useless, because they don't like to believe it is true. An evil lifestyle must always raise an objection to this book. Men question the truth of Christianity because they hate the practice of it.

Young men, when did God ever fail to keep His Word? Never. What He has said, He has always done; and what He has spoken, He has always made good. Did He fail to keep His Word at the flood? No. Did He fail with Sodom and Gomorrah? No. Did He fail with unbelieving Jerusalem? No. Has He failed with the Jews up to this very hour? No. He has never failed to fulfill His Word. Take care, lest you be found among those who despise God's Word.

Never laugh at Christianity. Never make a joke of

sacred things. Never mock those who are serious and earnest about their souls. The time may come when you will count those happy whom you laughed at – a time when your laughter will be turned into sorrow, and your mockery into seriousness.

(5) Another danger to young men is the fear of man's opinion.

The fear of man brings a snare (Proverbs 29:25). It is terrible to observe the power which it has over most minds, and especially over the minds of the young. Few seem to have any opinions of their own or to think for themselves. Like dead fish, they go with the stream and tide: what others think is right, they think is right; and what others call wrong, they call wrong too. There are not many original thinkers in the world. Most men are like sheep – they follow a leader. If it was the fashion of the day to be Roman Catholics, they would be Roman Catholics; if it was to be Islamic, they would be Islamic. They dread the idea of going against the current of the times. In a word, the opinion of the day becomes their religion, their creed, their Bible, and their God.

The thought of, *What will my friends say or think of me?* nips many a good inclination in the bud. The fear of being looked at, laughed at, and ridiculed prevents many a good habit from being taken up. There are Bibles that would be read this very day if the owners dared. They know they ought to read them, but they are afraid. "What will people say?" There are knees that would be bent in prayer this very night, but the fear of man forbids it. "What would my wife, my brother, my friend, my companion say if they saw me praying?" Oh, what wretched slavery this is, and yet how common! *I feared the people and consented unto their voice*, Saul said to Samuel, and so he *transgressed the commandment of the LORD* (1 Samuel 15:24). *I am afraid of the Jews*, said Zedekiah, the graceless king of Judah, and so he disobeyed the advice which Jeremiah gave him (Jeremiah 38:19). Herod was afraid of what his guests would think of him, so he did that which made him *exceeding sorry* – he beheaded John the Baptist. Pilate feared offending the Jews, so he did that which he knew in his conscience was unjust – he delivered up Jesus to be crucified. If this is not slavery, what is?

Young men, I want you all to be free from this bondage. I want each of you to care nothing about man's opinion, when the path of duty is clear. Believe me, it is a great thing to be able to say no! Here was good King Jehoshaphat's weak point – he was too easy and yielding in his dealings with Ahab and therefore caused many of his troubles (1 Kings 22:4). Learn to say no! Don't let the fear of not seeming to be good-natured make you unable to do it. When sinners entice you, be able to say decidedly, I will *not consent* (Proverbs 1:10).

Consider how unreasonable this fear of man is. How short-lived is man's hostility, and how little harm he can do you! *Who art thou that thou should be afraid of man that is mortal and of the son of man which shall be counted as stubble? And thou hast already forgotten the LORD thy maker that has stretched forth the heavens and laid the foundations of the earth* (Isaiah 51:12-13). And how thankless is this fear! No one will really think better of you for it. The world always respects those the most who act boldly for God. Oh, break these bonds and cast these chains from you! Never be ashamed of letting men see that you want to go to heaven. Do not think it a disgrace to show that you are a servant of God. Never be afraid of doing what is right.

> How short-lived is man's hostility, and how little harm he can do you!

Remember the words of the Lord Jesus: *And fear not those who kill the body but are not able to kill the soul, but rather fear him who is able to destroy both soul and body in hell* (Matthew 10:28). Try only to please God, and He will soon make others pleased with you. *When a man's ways please the LORD, he makes even his enemies to be at peace with him* (Proverbs 16:7). Young men, be of good courage. Don't worry about what the world says or thinks; you will not always be with the world. Can man save your soul? No. Will man be your judge in the great and dreadful day of judgment? No. Can man give you a good conscience in this life, a good hope in death, a good answer in the morning of resurrection? No! No! No! Man can do nothing of the sort. Then *do not fear the reproach of men, neither be afraid of their revilings. For the moth shall eat them up like a garment, and the worm shall eat them like wool* (Isaiah 51:7-8). Call to mind the saying of Gardiner: "I fear God, and therefore I have no one else to fear." Go and be like him.

Such are the warnings I give you. Take them to heart. They are worth thinking about. I am greatly mistaken if they are not greatly needed. The Lord grant that they have not been given to you in vain.

3

Some General Advice for Young Men

In the third place, I wish to give some general counsel to young men.

(1) Try to get a clear view of the evil of sin.

Young men, if you did know what sin is, and what sin has done, you would not think it so strange that I exhort you as I do. But you do not see it in its true colors. Your eyes are naturally blind to its guilt and danger, and therefore you cannot understand what makes me so worried about you. Oh, don't let the devil succeed in persuading you that sin is a small matter!

Think for a moment what the Bible says about sin: how it dwells naturally in the heart of every man and woman alive (Ecclesiastes 7:20; Romans 3:23); how it defiles our thoughts, words, and actions continually

(Genesis 6:5; Matthew 15:19); how it renders us all guilty and abominable in the sight of a holy God (Isaiah 64:6; Habakkuk 1:13); how it leaves us utterly without hope of salvation if we look to ourselves (Psalm 143:2; Romans 3:20); and how its fruit in this world is shame, and its wages in the world to come are death (Romans 6:21, 23). Think calmly about all this. I tell you this day, it is just as sad to be dying of cancer and not knowing it, as it is to be a living man and not know it.

Think what an awful change sin has worked on all our natures. Man is no longer what he was when God formed him out of the dust of the ground. He came out of God's hand upright and sinless (Ecclesiastes 7:29). In the day of his creation he was, like everything else, *very good* (Genesis 1:31). And what is man now? A fallen creature, a ruin, a being that shows the marks of corruption all over; his heart like Nebuchadnezzar, degraded and earthly, looking down and not up; his affections like a household in disorder, calling no man master, all extravagance and confusion; his understanding like a lamp flickering in the socket, impotent to guide him, not knowing good from evil; and his will like a rudderless ship, tossed to and fro by every desire, and constant only in choosing any way rather than God's. What a wreck man is, compared to what he might have been! We may understand such figures being used as blindness, deafness, disease, sleep, and death when the

Spirit has to give us a picture of man as he is. And man as he is, remember, was made so by sin.

Think too what it has cost to make atonement for sin and to provide a pardon and forgiveness for sinners. God's own Son had to come into the world and take upon Himself our due punishment, in order to pay the price of our redemption and deliver us from the curse of a broken law. He who was in the beginning with the Father, and by whom all things were made, must suffer for sin, the just for the unjust, and must die the death of a criminal before the way to heaven can be laid open to any soul. See the Lord Jesus Christ despised and rejected of men, scourged, mocked, and insulted; look at Him bleeding on the cross of Calvary; and hear Him crying in agony, "My God, my God, why have you forsaken me?" Note how the sun was darkened, and the rocks shook at the sight; and then consider, young men, what must be the evil and guilt of sin.

Think also of what sin has already done on the earth. Think how it threw Adam and Eve out of Eden, brought the flood upon the old world, caused fire to come down on Sodom and Gomorrah, drowned Pharaoh and his army in the Red Sea, destroyed the seven wicked nations of Canaan, and scattered the twelve tribes of Israel over the face of the earth. Sin alone did all this.

Think, moreover, of all the misery and sorrow that sin has caused, and is causing, to this very day. Pain, disease, death, strife, quarrels, divisions, envy, jealousy, malice, deceit, fraud, cheating, violence, oppression, robbery, selfishness, unkindness, and ingratitude – all these are the fruits of sin. Sin is the parent of them all. It is sin that has so marred and spoiled the face of God's creation.

Young men, consider these things, and you will not wonder why I say the things I'm saying. Surely, if you did think of these things, you would break with sin forever. Will you play with poison? Will you sport with hell? Will you take fire in your hand? Will you harbor your deadliest enemy in your arms? Will you go on living as if it mattered nothing whether your sins were forgiven or not, whether sin had dominion over you, or you over sin? Oh, wake up to a sense of sin's sinfulness and danger! Remember the words of Solomon: *Fools speak sin unto themselves, but among the righteous there is love* (Proverbs 14:9).

> If you would have your soul saved, then get up and pray.

Hear then the request that I make of you this day, and pray that God would teach you the real evil of sin. If you would have your soul saved, then get up and pray.

(2) Seek to become acquainted with our Lord Jesus Christ.

This is indeed the principal thing in Christianity.

This is the cornerstone of Christianity. Till you know this, my warnings and advice will be useless, and your endeavors, whatever they may be, will be in vain. A watch that does not keep time is as useless as religion without Christ.

But don't let me be misunderstood. It is not the mere knowing of Christ's name that I mean; it is the knowing of His mercy, grace, and power, the knowing of Him not by the hearing of the ear but by the experience of your hearts. I want you to know Him by faith. I want you, as Paul says, to know *the power of his resurrection . . . being made conformable unto his death* (Philippians 3:10). I want you to be able to say of Him, He is my peace and my strength, my life and my consolation, my Physician and my Shepherd, my Savior and my God.

Why do I make such a point of this? I do it because in Christ alone *all [God's] fullness dwell[s]* (Colossians 1:19), because in Him alone there is a full supply of all that we require for the needs of our souls. Of ourselves we are all poor, empty creatures, empty of righteousness and peace, empty of strength and comfort, empty of courage and patience, empty of power to stand or go on, or to make progress in this evil world. It is in Christ alone that all these things are to be found – grace, peace, wisdom, righteousness, sanctification, and redemption. It is just in proportion as we live upon

Him that we are strong Christians. It is only when self is nothing and Christ is all our confidence that we shall do great exploits. Only then are we armed for the battle of life and shall overcome. Only then are we prepared for the journey of life and shall move forward. To live on Christ, to draw all from Christ, to do all in the strength of Christ, to be ever looking to Christ – this is the true secret of spiritual prosperity. *I can do all things*, says Paul, *through Christ who strengthens me* (Philippians 4:13).

Young men, I set before you Jesus Christ this day, as the treasury of your souls, and I invite you to begin by going to Him. Let this be your first step – go to Christ. Do you want to consult friends? He is the best friend *that sticks closer than a brother* (Proverbs 18:24). Do you feel unworthy because of your sins? Do not fear; His blood cleanses from all sin. He says, *If your sins were as scarlet, they shall be made as white as snow; if they were red like crimson, they shall become as wool* (Isaiah 1:18). Do you feel weak and unable to follow Him? Do not fear; He will give you the power to become sons of God. He will give you the Holy Spirit to live in you and seal you for His own. He will give you a new heart, and He will put a new spirit within you. Are you troubled or beset with a strange bent to evil? Do not fear; there is no evil spirit that Jesus cannot cast out; there is no disease of soul that He cannot heal. Do you feel doubts and fears? Throw them aside. He says, *He that comes to me I will in no wise cast out* (John 6:37). He knows very well the heart of a young man. He knows your trials and your temptations, your difficulties and your foes. In the days of His flesh He was like you – a young man at Nazareth. He knows by experience a young man's mind. He can understand the feeling of your temptations because He Himself suffered when He was tempted. Surely, you will be without excuse if you turn away from such a Savior and friend as this.

Hear the request I make of you this day: if you love life, seek to become acquainted with Jesus Christ.

(3) Never forget that nothing is so important as your soul.

Your soul is eternal. It will live forever. The world and all that it contains will pass away – firm, solid, beautiful, well-ordered as it is, the world will come to an end. *The heavens shall pass away with a great noise, and the elements, burning, shall be dissolved, and the earth and the works that are in it shall be burned up* (2 Peter 3:10).

> Try, I beg you, to realize the fact that your soul is the one thing worth living for.

The works of statesmen, writers, painters, and architects are all short-lived; your soul will outlive them all. The angel's voice shall proclaim one day *that there should be time no longer* (Revelation 10:6). Try, I beg you, to realize the fact that your soul is the one thing worth living for. It is the part of you which ought always to be considered first. No place, no employment is good for you which injures your soul. No friend, no companion deserves your confidence who makes light of your soul's concerns. The man who hurts you, your property, or your character only does you temporary harm. Your true Enemy is the one who plots to damage your soul.

Think for a moment about why you were born into the world. Not merely to eat and drink and indulge the desires of the flesh, not merely to dress up your body and follow its lusts wherever they may lead you, not merely to work, sleep, laugh, talk, and enjoy yourselves and think of nothing but time. No! You were meant for something higher and better than this. You were placed here to train for eternity. Your body was only intended to be a house for your immortal spirit. It is flying in the face of God's purposes to do as many do – to make the soul a servant to the body and not the body a servant to the soul.

Young men, God does not show favoritism nor respects the honors bestowed by men. He rewards no man's heritage, or wealth, or rank, or position. He does not see with man's eyes. The poorest saint that ever died in a ghetto is nobler in His sight than the richest sinner that ever died in a palace. God does not look at riches, titles, education, beauty, or anything of the kind. There is only one thing that God does look at, and that is the immortal soul. He measures all men by one standard, one measure, one test, and one criterion, and that is the state of their souls.

Do not forget this. Keep it in view morning, noon, and night – the interests of your soul. Rise up each day desiring that your soul may excel, and lie down each evening asking yourself whether your soul has really grown. Set your immortal soul before your mind's eye, and when men ask you why you live as you do, answer them in his spirit, "I live for my soul." Believe me, the day is fast coming when the soul will be the one thing men will think of, and the only question of importance will be this: "Is my soul lost or saved?"

(4) Remember it is possible to be a young man and yet serve God.

I fear the snares that Satan lays for you on this point. I fear that he will succeed in filling your minds with the vain notion that to be a true Christian as a youth is impossible. I have seen many carried away by this delusion. I have heard it said, "You are requiring an impossibility in expecting so much Christianity from young people. Youth is no time for seriousness. Our desires are strong, and it was never intended that we should keep them under such strong Christian control as you wish us to do. God meant for us to enjoy ourselves. There will be plenty of time for religion in the future." And this kind of talk is only too much encouraged by the world. The world is only too ready to wink at youthful sins. The world appears to think it a matter of course that young men must "sow their wild oats." The world seems to take it for granted that young people must be irreligious and that it is not possible for them to follow Christ.

Young men, I will ask you this simple question: Where will you find anything of this in the Word of God? Where is the chapter or verse in the Bible which will support this talking and reasoning of the world? Doesn't the Bible speak to old and young alike without distinction? Is not sin, sin – whether committed at the age of twenty or fifty? Will it form the slightest excuse in the day of judgment to say, "I know I sinned, but I was young then"? Show your common sense, I beg of you, by giving up such vain excuses. You are responsible and accountable to God from the very moment that you know right and wrong.

I know very well that there are many difficulties in a man's way. But there are always difficulties in the way of doing right. The path to heaven is always narrow, whether we be young or old. There are difficulties, but God will give you the grace to overcome them. God is no hard master. He will not, like Pharaoh, require you to make bricks without straw. He will make sure that

SOME GENERAL ADVICE FOR YOUNG MEN

the path He requires us to walk on is never an impossible road. He never gave commands to man which He would not give man the power to perform.

There are difficulties, but many a young man has overcome them in the past, and so can you. Moses was a young man with passions like yourself; but see what is said of him in Scripture: *By faith Moses, when he was come to years, refused to be called the son of Pharaoh's daughter, choosing rather to suffer affliction with the people of God than to enjoy the pleasures of sin for a season, esteeming the reproach of the Christ greater riches than the treasures in Egypt, for he had respect unto the recompense of the reward* (Hebrews 11:24-26). Daniel was a young man when he began to serve God in Babylon. He was surrounded by temptations of every kind. He had few people with him and many against him. Yet Daniel's life was so blameless and consistent that even his enemies could not find any fault in him, *except we find it against him in the law of his God* (Daniel 6:5). And these are not solitary cases. There is a cloud of witnesses whom I could name. Time would not allow me, if I were to tell you of young Isaac, young Joseph, young Joshua, young Samuel, young David, young Solomon, young Abijah, young Obadiah, young Josiah, and young Timothy.

> There are difficulties, but many a young man has overcome them in the past, and so can you.

These were not angels, but men, with natural hearts like your own. They too had obstacles to contend with, lusts to mortify, trials to endure, and hard places to travel like any of you. But young as they were, they all found it possible to serve God. Will they not all rise in judgment and condemn you if you persist in saying it cannot be done?

Young men, try to serve God. Resist the devil when he whispers it is impossible. Try, and the Lord God of the promises will give you strength in the trying. He loves to meet those who struggle to come to Him, and He will meet you and give you the power that you feel you need. Be like the man whom Bunyan's Pilgrim saw in the Interpreter's house: go forward boldly, saying, "Write down my name." These words of our Lord are true, though I often hear them repeated by heartless and unfeeling tongues: *Seek, and ye shall find; knock, and it shall be opened unto you* (Matthew 7:7).

Difficulties which seemed like mountains shall melt away like snow in spring. Obstacles which seemed like giants in the distance will dwindle into nothing when you actually face them. The lion that blocks the way that you are traveling and causes you great fear will prove to be chained and unable to harm you. If men believed the promises more, they would never be afraid of their assigned duties. But remember that little word I press upon you, and when Satan says, "You cannot be a Christian while you are young," answer him, "Get behind me, Satan. By God's help, I will try."

(5) Determine as long as you live to make the Bible your guide and adviser.

The Bible is God's merciful provision for sinful man's soul, the map by which he must steer his course if he would attain eternal life. All that we need to know in order to make us peaceful, holy, or happy is richly contained there. If a young man wants to know how to begin his life well, let him hear what David says: *With what shall a young man cleanse his way? when he shall keep thy word* (Psalm 119:9).

Young men, I charge you to make a habit of reading the Bible, and not to let the habit be broken. Do not let the laughter of friends, do not let the bad customs of the family you live in, do not let any of these things prevent you from doing it. Determine that you will not only have a Bible, but that you will also make time to read it. Allow no man to persuade you that it is only a book for Sunday school children and old women. It is the book from which King David got wisdom and understanding. It is the book which young Timothy knew from his childhood. Never be ashamed of reading it. Do not *despise the word* (Proverbs 13:13).

Read it with the prayer that the Holy Spirit's grace will help you understand it. It has been said that a man may just as soon read the Scripture without eyes, as understand the spirit of it without grace.

Read it reverently, as the Word of God, not of man, believing implicitly that what it approves is right, and what it condemns is wrong. Be very sure that every doctrine which will not stand the test of Scripture is false. This will keep you from being tossed to and fro and carried about by the dangerous opinions of these latter days. Be very sure that every practice in your life which is contrary to Scripture is sinful and must be given up. This will settle many a question of conscience and cut the knot of many a doubt. Remember how differently two kings of Judah read the Word of God: Jehoiakim read it, and at once tore the page to pieces, and burned it in the fire (Jeremiah 36:32). And why? Because his heart rebelled against it, and he was resolved not to obey. Josiah read it, and at once tore his clothes, and cried mightily to the Lord (2 Chronicles 34:19). And why? Because his heart was tender and obedient. He was ready to do anything which Scripture showed him was his duty. Oh, that you may follow the last of these two and not the first!

And read it regularly. This is the only way to become mighty in the Scriptures. A quick glance at the Bible now and then does little good. At that rate you will never become familiar with its treasures or feel the sword of the Spirit fitted to your hand in the hour of conflict. But store up your mind with Scripture, by diligent reading, and you will soon discover its value and power. Texts will rise up in your heart in the moment of temptation. Commands will suggest themselves in times of doubt. Promises will come across your thoughts in the time of discouragement. And thus you will experience the truth of David's words, *Thy spoken word have I hid in my heart that I might not sin against thee* (Psalm 119:11), and of Solomon's words, *When thou goest, it shall lead thee; when thou sleepest, it shall keep thee; and when thou wakest, it shall talk with thee* (Proverbs 6:22).

I dwell on these things more because this is an age of reading. There seems to be no end to the producing of many books, though few of them are really profitable. There seems a rage for cheap printing and publishing. Media of every sort abounds, and the tone of some, which have the widest circulation, speaks badly for the taste of the age. Amid the flood of dangerous reading, I plead for my Master's Book; I call upon you not to forget the book of the soul. Do not let newspapers, novels, and romances be read while the prophets and apostles be despised. Do not let the exciting and sensual swallow up your attention, while the edifying and the sanctifying can find no place in your mind.

> Amid the flood of dangerous reading, I plead for my Master's Book.

Young men, give the Bible the honor due it every day you live. Whatever you read, read that first. And beware of bad books; there are plenty in this day. Take heed what you read. I suspect there is more harm done to souls in this way than most people have an idea is possible. Value all books in proportion as they are agreeable to Scripture. Those that are nearest to it are the best, and those that are farthest from it, and most contrary to it, are the worst.

(6) Never make an intimate friend of anyone who is not a friend of God.

Understand me, I do not speak of acquaintances. I do not mean that you ought to have nothing to do with anyone except true Christians. To take such a line is neither possible nor desirable in this world. Christianity requires no man to be discourteous.

But I do advise you to be very careful in your choice of friends. Do not open all your heart to a man merely because he is clever, agreeable, good-natured, and kind. These things are all very well in their way, but they are not everything. Never be satisfied with the friendship of anyone who will not be useful to your soul.

Believe me, the importance of this advice cannot be overrated. There is no telling the harm that is done by associating with godless companions and friends. The devil has few better helpers in ruining a man's soul. Grant him this help, and he cares little for all the armor with which you may be armed against him. Good education, early habits of morality, sermons, books, all he knows well will avail you little if you only cling to ungodly friends. You may resist many open temptations and refuse many plain snares, but once you take up a bad companion, he is content. That awful chapter which describes Amnon's wicked conduct with Tamar almost begins with these words: *But Amnon had a friend, . . . a very astute man* (2 Samuel 13:3).

You must remember, we are all creatures of imitation. Precept may teach us, but it is example that draws us. There is that in us all, that we are always disposed to catch the ways of those with whom we live, and the more we like them, the stronger does the disposition grow. Without our being aware of it, they influence our tastes and opinions; we gradually give up what they dislike and take up what they like in order to become closer friends with them. And, worst of all, we catch their ways in things that are wrong far quicker than in things that are right. Health, unfortunately, is not contagious, but disease is. It is much easier to catch a chill than to impart a warmth, and to make each other's religion dwindle away than grow and prosper.

Young men, I ask you to take these things to heart. Before you let anyone become your constant companion, before you get into the habit of telling him everything and going to him with all your troubles and all your pleasures – before you do this, just think of what I have been saying, and ask yourself, will this be a useful friendship to me or not?

Evil companions corrupt good character (1 Corinthians 15:33). I wish that text were written in the hearts of all young men. Good friends are among our greatest blessings; they may keep us away from much evil, remind us of our course, speak an appropriate word at the right time, draw us upward, and draw us on. But a bad friend is a burden, a weight continually dragging us down and chaining us to earth. Keep company with an unsaved man, and it is more than probable you will in the end become like him. That is the general consequence of all such friendships. The good go down to the bad, and the bad do not come up to the good. The world's proverbs are only too correct: "Clothes and company tell true tales about character." "Show me who a man lives with and I will show you what he is."

I dwell upon this point because it has more to do with your prospects in life than it first appears. If you ever marry, it is more than probable you will choose a wife from among your circle of friends or their acquaintances. If Jehoshaphat's son Jehoram had not formed a friendship with Ahab's family, he would most likely not have married Ahab's daughter. And who can estimate the importance of a right choice in marriage? It is a step which, according to the old saying, "either makes a man or ruins him." Your happiness in both lives may depend on it. Your wife must either help your soul or harm it. She will either fan the flame of Christianity in your heart, or throw cold water upon it and make it burn low. She will either be wings or handcuffs, an encouragement or a hindrance to your Christianity, according to her character. He that finds a good wife does indeed find a good thing; so if you have the desire to find one, be very careful how you choose your friends.

Do you ask me what kind of friends you should choose? Choose friends who will benefit your soul, friends whom you can really respect, friends whom you would like to have near you on your deathbed, friends who love the Bible and are not afraid to speak to you about it, and friends whom you would not be ashamed of having at the coming of Christ and the day of judgment. Follow the example that David sets for you. He says, *I am a companion of all those that fear thee and of those that keep thy precepts* (Psalm 119:63). Remember the words of Solomon: *He that walks with wise men shall be wise, but the companion of fools shall be destroyed* (Proverbs 13:20). But depend on it, bad company in this life is the sure way to procure worse company in the life to come.

4

Special Rules of Conduct for Young Men

In the last place, I will set down some particular rules of conduct which I strongly advise all young men to follow.

(1) Resolve at once, by God's help, to break off every known sin, however small.

Look within, each one of you. Examine your own hearts. Do you see there any habit or custom which you know is wrong in the sight of God? If you do, don't delay for a moment in attacking it. Resolve at once to lay it aside. Nothing darkens the eyes of the mind so much, and deadens the conscience so surely, as an allowed sin. It may be a little one, but it is not any less dangerous. A small leak will sink a great ship, a small spark will kindle a great fire, and a little allowed sin in like manner will ruin an immortal soul. Take my advice, and never spare a little sin. Israel was commanded to kill every Canaanite, both great and small. Act on the same principle, and show no mercy to little sins. Well says the book of the Song of Solomon, *Hunt the foxes for us, the little foxes, that spoil the vines* (Song of Solomon 2:15).

You can be sure that no wicked man ever meant to be so wicked at his first beginnings. But he began with allowing himself some little sins, and that led to something greater, and that in time produced something greater still, and thus he became the miserable being that he now is. When Hazael heard from Elisha of the horrible acts that he would one day do, he said with astonishment, *But what, is thy slave a dog, that he should do this great thing?* (2 Kings 8:13). But he allowed sin to take root in his heart, and in the end he did them all.

Young men, resist sin in its beginnings. It may look small and insignificant, but mind what I say, resist it, make no compromise, and let no sin lodge quietly and undisturbed in your heart. There is nothing finer than the point of a needle, but when it has made a hole, it draws all the thread after it. Remember the apostle's words: *A little leaven leavens the whole lump* (1 Corinthians 5:6).

Many a young man could tell you, with sorrow

and shame, that he traces the ruin of all his worldly prospects to the point I speak of – to giving way to sin in its beginnings. He began habits of deception and dishonesty in little things, and they grew on him. Step by step, he has gone from bad to worse, till he has done things that at one time he would have thought impossible, till at last he has lost his standing, lost his character, lost his peace, and almost lost his soul. He allowed a gap in the wall of his conscience, because it seemed a little one, and once allowed, that gap grew larger every day, till in time the whole wall seemed to come down.

> Whatever the world may like to think, there are no little sins.

Remember this especially in matters of truth and honesty. Be careful in even the smallest syllable spoken. *He that is faithful with little is faithful also with much* (Luke 16:10). Whatever the world may like to think, there are no little sins. All great buildings are made up of little parts – the first stone is as important as any other. All habits are formed by a succession of little acts, and the first little act is of mighty consequence. The axe in the fable only begged the trees to let him have one little piece of wood to make a handle, and he would never trouble them anymore. He got it, and then he soon cut them all down. The devil only wants to get the wedge of a little allowed sin into your heart, and you will soon be all his own. It is a wise saying: "There is nothing small between us and God, for God is an infinite God."

There are two ways of coming down from the top of a ladder: one is to jump down, and the other is to come down by the steps. But both will lead you to the bottom. So also there are two ways of going to hell: one is to walk into it with your eyes open – few people do that; the other is to go down by the steps of little sins – and that way, I fear, is only too common. Put up with a few little sins, and you will soon want a few more. Even a heathen could say, "Who was ever content with only one sin?" If you put up with little sins, then your path in life will be worse and worse every year. Jeremy Taylor very clearly described the progress of sin in a man:

"First, it startles him, then it becomes pleasing, then easy, then delightful, then frequent, then habitual, then a way of life! Then the man feels no guilt, then is obstinate, then resolves never to repent, and then he is damned."

Young men, if you don't want to come to this, remember the rule I give you this day – resolve at once to break off every known sin.

(2) Resolve, by God's help, to shun everything which may prove an occasion of sin.

It is an excellent saying, "He that would be safe from the acts of evil must widely avoid the occasions." There is an old fable, that the butterfly once asked the owl how she should deal with the fire which had singed her wings; and the owl counseled her, in reply, not to even look at its smoke. It is not enough that we determine not to commit sin; we must carefully keep at a distance from all approaches to it. By this test we ought to examine the ways we spend our time – the books that we read, the friends that we visit, the part of society which we interact with. We must not be content with saying, "There is nothing wrong here"; we must go further and say, "Is there anything here which may cause me to sin?"

This is one great reason why idleness is to be avoided. It is not that doing nothing is of itself so wicked; it is the opportunity it affords to evil and empty thoughts; it is the wide door it opens for Satan to throw in the seeds of bad things; it is this which is mainly to be feared. If David had not given opportunity to the devil by walking on his housetop in Jerusalem with nothing to do, he probably never would have seen Bathsheba bathing, nor murdered her husband, Uriah.

This too is one good reason why worldly entertainments are so objectionable. It may be difficult, in some instances, to show that they are, in themselves, positively unscriptural and wrong. But there is little difficulty in showing that the tendency of almost all of them is most injurious to the soul. They sow the seeds of an earthly and sensual frame of mind. They war against the life of faith. They promote an unhealthy and unnatural craving after excitement. They minister to the lust of the flesh and the lust of the eye and the pride of life. They dim the view of heaven and eternity, and give a false color to the things of time. They take away time for private prayer, Scripture reading, and calm communion with God. The man who mingles in them is like one who gives Satan an advantage. He has a battle to fight, and he gives his Enemy the help of sun, wind, and hill. It would indeed be strange if he did not find himself continually overcome.

Young men, endeavor as much as you can to keep clear of everything which may prove injurious to your soul. People may say you are too conscientious, too particular, and ask where is the great harm of such and such things. But don't listen to them. It is dangerous to play tricks with sharp tools; it is far more dangerous to take liberties with your immortal soul. He that would be safe must not come near the brink of danger. He must look on his heart as a barrel of gunpowder, and be cautious not to handle one spark of temptation more than he can help.

What is the use of your praying, "Lord, keep me from temptation," unless you are careful not to run into it; and "keep me from evil," unless you show a desire to keep out of its way? Take an example from Joseph: not merely did he refuse solicitation to sin from his master's wife, but he also showed his prudence in refusing to even *be with her* (Genesis 39:10). Take to heart the advice of Solomon, not only to *enter not into the path of the wicked,* but also to *avoid it, pass not by it, turn from it, and pass away* (Proverbs 4:14-15), and *Do not look upon the wine when it is red, when it gives its colour in the cup, it goes down smoothly* (Proverbs 23:31). The man who took the vow of a Nazarite in Israel not only took no wine, but also even abstained from grapes in any shape whatsoever. *Abhor that which is evil,* says Paul to the Romans (Romans 12:9), not merely not *do* evil. *Flee youthful lusts,* he writes to Timothy; get away from them as far as possible (2 Timothy 2:22). Oh, how needful are such cautions! Dinah just had to go out among the wicked Shechemites to see their ways, and she lost her virginity. Lot just had to pitch his tent near sinful Sodom, and he lost everything but his life.

Young men, be wise with your time. Do not always be trying to see how near you can allow the Enemy of souls to come and yet escape him. Hold him at arm's length. Try to keep clear of temptation as far as possible, and this will be one great help to keep clear of sin.

(3) Resolve never to forget the eye of God.

The eye of God! Think of that. Everywhere, in every house, in every field, in every room, in every company, alone or in a crowd, the eye of God is always on you. *The eyes of the LORD are in every place, beholding those who are evil and those who are good* (Proverbs 15:3), and they are eyes that read hearts as well as actions.

Endeavor, I beg you, to realize this fact. Remember that you have to deal with an all-seeing God, a God who never sleeps, a God who understands your thoughts and with whom the night shines as the day. You may leave your father's house and go away, like the prodigal, into a far country, and think that there is nobody to watch your conduct; but the eyes and ears of God are there before you. You may deceive your parents or employers; you may tell them lies and act one way before their faces and another way behind their backs, but you cannot deceive God. He knows you through and through. He heard everything you said so far today. He knows what you are thinking at this minute. He has set your most secret sins in the light of His countenance, and they will one day come out before the world to your shame, unless you take heed.

How little is this really felt! How many things are

done continually which men would never do if they thought they were seen! How many matters are transacted in the rooms of imagination which would never bear the light of day! Yes, men entertain thoughts in private, and say words in private, and do acts in private, which they would be ashamed and blush to have exposed before the world. The sound of a footstep coming has stopped many a deed of wickedness. A knock at the door has caused many an evil work to be hastily suspended and hurriedly laid aside. But oh, what miserable folly is all this! There is an all-seeing Witness with us wherever we go. Lock the door, pull down the blind, turn out the light. It doesn't matter, it makes no difference; God is everywhere, and you cannot shut Him out or prevent His seeing. *Neither is there any created thing that is not manifested in his presence, but all things are naked and opened unto the eyes of him of whom we speak* (Hebrews 4:13). Young Joseph understood this well when his employer's wife tempted him. There was no one in the house to see them, no human eye to witness against him; but Joseph was one who lived as seeing Him who is invisible: *How then can I do this great wickedness and sin against God?* (Genesis 39:9).

Young men, I ask all of you to read Psalm 139. I advise all of you to learn it by heart. Make it the test of all your dealings in this world's business. Say to yourself often, "Do I remember that God sees me?"

Live as in the sight of God. This is what Abraham did; he walked before Him. This is what Enoch did; he walked with Him. This is what heaven itself will be, the eternal presence of God. Do nothing that you would not like God to see. Say nothing you would not like God to hear. Write nothing you would not like God to read. Go no place where you would not like God to find you. Read no book of which you would not like God to say, "Show it to Me." Never spend your time in such a way that you would not like to have God say, "What are you doing?"

(4) Be diligent in the practice of your Christianity.

Be regular in going to church, whenever it is open for prayer and preaching and it is in your power to attend. Be regular in keeping the Lord's Day holy, and determine that God's day out of the seven shall always be given to its rightful owner.

I would not want to leave any false impression on your minds. Do not go away and say I told you that going to church made up the whole of Christianity. I will tell you no such thing. I have no wish to see you grow up to be formalists and Pharisees. If you think the mere carrying of your body to a certain building at certain times on a certain day in the week will make you a Christian and prepare you to meet God, I tell you flatly you are miserably deceived. All services without heart-service are unprofitable and vain. The only true worshipers are those who *worship the Father in spirit and in truth, for the Father seeks such to worship him* (John 4:23).

The practices of Christianity are not to be despised, even though it's not the practices themselves that save you. Gold is not food; you cannot eat it, but you would not say it is useless and throw it away. Your soul's eternal well-being most certainly does not depend on the practices of Christianity, but it is certain that without them, as a general rule, your soul will not do well. God could take all who are saved to heaven in a chariot of fire, as He did Elijah, but He does not do so. He could teach them all by visions and dreams and miraculous interventions, without requiring them to read or think for themselves, but He does not do so. And why not? Because He is a God who works by means, and it is His law and will that in all man's dealings with Him, means shall be used. No one but a fool would think of building a house without ladders and scaffolding, and just so, no wise man will despise the means and practice of Christianity.

I dwell on this point because Satan will try hard to fill your minds with arguments against the practices of Christianity. He will draw your attention to the numbers of persons who use them and are no better for the using. "See there," he will whisper, "do you not observe that those who go to church are no better than those who stay away?" But do not let this move you. It is never fair to argue against a thing because it is improperly used. It does not follow that the practices of Christianity can do no good because many do them and get no good from them. Medicine is not to be despised because many take it and do not recover their health. No man would think of giving up eating and drinking because others choose to eat and drink improperly and so make themselves sick. The value of the practices of Christianity, like other things, depends in great measure on the manner and spirit in which we use them.

I dwell on this point too because of the strong anxiety I feel that every young man should regularly hear the preaching of Christ's gospel. I cannot emphasize enough how important I think this is. By God's blessing, the ministry of the gospel might be the means of converting your soul, of leading you to a saving knowledge of Christ, and of making you a child of God in action and in truth. This would indeed be cause for eternal thankfulness. This would be an event over which angels would rejoice. But even if this were not the case, there is a restraining power and influence in the ministry of the gospel under which I earnestly desire every young man to be brought. There are thousands whom it keeps back from evil, though it has not yet turned them to God; it has made them far better members of society, though it has not yet made them true Christians. There is a certain kind of mysterious power in the faithful preaching of the gospel which has an effect on multitudes who listen to it without receiving it into their hearts. To hear sin exposed for what it is and holiness lifted up, to hear Christ exalted and the words of the devil denounced, to hear the kingdom of heaven and its blessedness described and the world and its emptiness exposed – to hear this week after week and Sunday after Sunday is seldom without a good effect on the soul. It makes it far harder afterwards to run out and commit gross sins. It acts as a wholesome check upon a man's heart. This, I believe, is one way in which that promise of God is made good: *So shall my Word be that goes forth out of my mouth: it shall not return unto me void* (Isaiah 55:11). There is so much truth in that strong saying of Whitefield: "The gospel keeps many a person from going to jail and from being hanged, if it does not keep him from hell."

Let me state another point which is closely connected to this subject. Let nothing ever tempt you to become a Christian which does not allow you to make every effort to attend church on Sunday and make the day special to the Lord. Make up your mind to give all your Sundays to God. A spirit of disregard for this day is growing up among us with fearful rapidity, and not least among young men. Sunday vacations, Sunday visiting, and Sunday excursions to the exclusion of church attendance and honoring of the Lord are becoming more common every year than they were before and are doing infinite harm to souls.

Young men, be jealous on this point. Whether you live in the city or in the country, take up a decided line: resolve not to miss church on Sunday and the fellowship of God's people. Do not let the plausible argument of needing to sleep in to rest your body, do not let not the example of all those around you, and do not let the invitation of companions pull you away from fellowship and worship. Let none of these things move you to depart from this settled rule, that Sundays are for God's honor and for fellowship with His people.

Once you don't consider Sundays important or as anything special in your Christian life, then in the end you will give up caring for your soul. The steps which lead to this conclusion are easy and common. Begin with not honoring the Lord's Day, and you will soon not honor God's people; cease to honor God's Book, and in time you will give God no honor at all. Let a man lay the foundation of having no respect for God's worship or the fellowship of the saints, and I am never surprised if he finishes with no God. It is a remarkable saying of Judge Hale: "Of all the persons who were convicted of capital crimes while he was on the bench, he found only a few who would not confess, on inquiry, that they began their career of wickedness by a neglect of the church and God's people."

Young men, you may have friends who forget the honor of the Lord's Day, but resolve, by God's help, that you will always remember to keep it special. Honor it by a regular attendance at some place where the gospel is preached. Settle down under a faithful ministry, and once settled, let your place in church never be empty. Believe me, you will find a special blessing following you: *If thou turn away thy foot from the sabbath, from doing thy will on my holy day; and call the sabbath the delightful, holy, glorious day of the LORD; and shalt honour him by not doing thine own ways, nor seeking thine own will, nor speaking thine own words: Then shalt thou delight thyself in the LORD; and I will cause thee to ride upon the high places of the earth and cause thee to eat of the heritage of Jacob thy father* (Isaiah 58:13-14). And one thing is very certain: your feelings about Sunday and the fellowship will always be a test and criterion of your fitness for heaven. Fellowship and worship are a foretaste and a fragment of heaven. The man who finds them a burden and not a privilege may be sure that his heart stands in need of a mighty change.

(5) Resolve that wherever you are, you will pray.

Prayer is the life-breath of a man's soul. Without it, we may have a name to live, and be counted Christians, but we are dead in the sight of God. The feeling that we must cry to God for mercy and peace is a mark of salvation; and the habit of spreading before Him our soul's needs is an evidence that we have the spirit of adoption. And prayer is the appointed way to obtain the relief of our spiritual necessities. It opens the treasury and sets the fountain flowing. If we don't have, it is because we don't ask.

Prayer is the way to procure the outpouring of the Spirit upon our hearts. Jesus has promised the Holy Spirit, the Comforter. He is ready to come down with all His precious gifts, renewing, sanctifying, purifying, strengthening, cheering, encouraging, enlightening, teaching, directing, and guiding into all truth. But He waits to be asked.

And here is where, I say it with sorrow, that men fall short so miserably. Few indeed are to be found who pray. There are many who go down on their knees and say a form perhaps, but few who pray. There are few who cry out to God, few who call on the Lord, few who seek as if they wanted to find, few who knock as if they hungered and thirsted, few who wrestle, few who strive with God earnestly for an answer, few who give Him no rest, few who continue in prayer, few who pray always without ceasing and do not grow weak. Yes, few pray! It is just one of the things assumed as a matter of course, but seldom practiced; it is a thing which is everybody's business, but in fact hardly anybody performs.

Young men, believe me, if your soul is to be saved, you must pray. God has no speechless children. If you are to resist the world, the flesh, and the devil, you must pray. It is in vain to look for strength in the hour of trial if it has not been sought for. You may be thrown in with those who never do it, you may have to sleep in the same room with someone who never asks anything of God; still, mark my words, you must pray.

> If you are to resist the world, the flesh, and the devil, you must pray.

I can believe that you find it difficult to do – difficult to find opportunities to pray, and times to pray, and places to pray. I dare not lay down too strict rules on such points as these. I leave them to your own conscience. Circumstances must guide you. Our Lord Jesus Christ prayed on a mountain; Isaac prayed in the fields; Hezekiah turned his face to the wall as he lay upon his bed; Daniel prayed by the riverside; Peter the apostle prayed on the housetop. I have heard of young men praying in stables and haylofts. All that I contend for is this: you must know what it is to *enter into thy chamber, and when thou hast shut thy door, pray to thy Father who is in secret* (Matthew 6:6). There must be stated times when you must speak to God face to face; you must every day have your times for prayer – you must pray.

Without this, all my advice and counsel is useless. This is that piece of spiritual armor that Paul names last in his list in Ephesians 6, but it is in truth first in value and importance. This is that meat which you must eat daily if you would travel safely through the wilderness of this life. It is only in the strength of this that you will get onward towards the mountain of God. I have heard it said that some people who grind metal sometimes wear a magnetic mouthpiece at their work, which catches all the fine metal dust that flies around them, prevents it from entering their lungs, and so saves their lives. Prayer is the mouthpiece that you must wear continually, or else you will never work uninjured by the unhealthy atmosphere of this sinful world. You must pray.

Young men, be sure no time is so well spent as that which a man spends on his knees. Make time for this, whatever your situation may be. Think of David, king of Israel; what does he say? *Evening and morning and at noon I will pray and cry aloud, and he shall hear my voice* (Psalm 55:17). Think of Daniel. He had all the business of a kingdom on his hands, yet he prayed three times a day. See there the secret of his safety in wicked Babylon. Think of Solomon. He begins his reign with prayer for help and assistance, and hence his wonderful prosperity. Think of Nehemiah. He could find time to pray to the God of heaven even when standing in the presence of his master, Artaxerxes. Think of the example these good men have left you, and go and do likewise.

Oh, that the Lord may give you all the spirit of grace and supplication! *Wilt thou not from this time cry unto me, My Father, thou art the guide of youth?* (Jeremiah 3:4). Gladly would I consent to the fact that all of this message may be forgotten, if only this doctrine of the importance of prayer might be impressed on your hearts.

5

Conclusion

And now we're coming to the end of my straightforward book. I have said things that many perhaps will not like and not receive, but I appeal to your consciences – are they not true?

Young men, you all have consciences. Corrupt and ruined by the fall as we are, each of us has a conscience. In a corner of each heart there sits a witness for God, a witness who condemns when we do wrong and approves when we do right. To that witness I make my appeal this day; are not the things that I have been saying true?

Go then, young men, and resolve this day to remember your Creator in the days of your youth. Before the day of grace is past, before your conscience has become hardened by age, and deadened by repeated trampling under foot, while you have strength and time and opportunities, go and join yourself to the Lord in an everlasting covenant not to be forgotten. The Spirit will not always strive. The voice of conscience will become feebler and fainter every year that you continue to resist it. The Athenians said to Paul, "We want to hear you again on this subject," but they had heard him for the last time (Acts 17:32). Make haste, and don't delay. Linger and hesitate no more.

Think of the unspeakable comfort you will give to parents, relatives, and friends if you take my counsel. They have expended time, money, and health to raise you and make you what you are. Surely they deserve some consideration. Who can know the joy and gladness which young people have in their power to give? Who can tell the anxiety and sorrow that sons like Esau, Hophni, Phinehas, and Absalom may cause? Truly indeed does Solomon say, *A wise son makes a glad father; but a foolish son is sadness unto his mother* (Proverbs 10:1). Oh, consider these things, and give God your heart! Let it not be said of you at last, as it is of many, that your youth was a disorder, your manhood a struggle, and your old age a regret.

Think of the good you might be doing for the world. Almost all the eminent saints of God sought the Lord early. Moses, Samuel, David, and Daniel all served God from their youth. God seems to delight in putting special honor upon young servants; and think of what we could expect if young men in our own

CONCLUSION

day would consecrate the springtime of their lives to God. Workers are wanted now in almost every great and good cause, and cannot be found. Technology of every kind for spreading truth exists, but there are not people to make it work.

Money is more easily obtained for doing good than men. Ministers are wanted for new churches, missionaries are wanted for new fields, teachers are wanted for Sunday school, and many a good cause is standing still merely for want of workers. The supply of godly, faithful, and trustworthy men for posts like those I have named is far below the demand.

Young men of the present day, you are wanted for God. This is an age of activity. We are shaking off some of our past selfishness. Men no longer sleep the sleep of apathy and indifference about others, as their forefathers did. They are beginning to be ashamed of thinking like Cain, "Am I my brother's keeper?" A wide field of usefulness is open before you, if you are only willing to enter into it. The harvest is great, and the workers are few. Be zealous for good works. Come, come to the aid of the Lord against the wickedness of this age.

> Young men of the present day, you are wanted for God.

This is, in some sort, to be like God – not only good, but also doing good (Psalm 119:68). This is the way to follow the steps of your Lord and Savior: He *went about doing good* (Acts 10:38).

And who can doubt that this is the path which makes an immortal soul beautiful? Who would not rather leave this world like Josiah, grieved by all, than depart like Jehoram, *without being desired* (2 Chronicles 21:20)? Is it better to be idle, frivolous, to live for your body, your selfishness, your lusts, and your pride, or to spend and be spent in the glorious cause of usefulness to your fellow men – to be a blessing to your country and the world, to be the friend of the prisoner and the captive, to be the spiritual father of hundreds of immortal souls in heathen lands, to be a burning and a shining light, an epistle of Christ, known and read of all men, the inspiration of every Christian heart that comes across your path? Oh, who can doubt? Who can for one moment doubt?

Young men, consider your responsibilities. Think of the privilege and luxury of doing good. Resolve this day to be useful. Give your hearts at once to Christ.

Lastly, think of the happiness that will come to your own soul if you serve God – happiness as you travel through life and happiness in the end, when the journey is over. Believe me, whatever vain notions you may have heard, there is a reward for the righteous even in this world. Godliness has indeed the promise of this life as well as of that which is to come. There is

CONCLUSION

a solid peace in feeling that God is your friend. There is a real satisfaction in knowing that however great your unworthiness, you are complete in Christ, you have an enduring portion, and you have chosen that good part which shall not be taken from you.

The backslider in heart may well be content with his own ways, but *the good man shall be separated from him* (Proverbs 14:14). The path of the worldly man grows darker and darker every year that he lives; the path of the Christian is like a shining light, growing brighter and brighter to the very end. His sun is just rising when the sun of the worldly is setting forever; his best things are all beginning to blossom and bloom forever when those of the worldly are all slipping out of his hands and passing away.

Young men, these things are true. Listen to the word of exhortation. Be persuaded. Take up the cross. Follow Christ. Yield yourselves to God.

J. C. Ryle – A Brief Biography

John Charles Ryle was born into a wealthy, affluent, socially elite family on May 10, 1816 – the firstborn son of John Ryle, a banker, and his wife Susanna (Wirksworth) Ryle. As the firstborn, John lived a privileged life and was set to inherit all of his father's estate and pursue a career in Parliament. His future promised to be planned and comfortable with no material needs.

J. C. Ryle attended a private school and then earned academic scholarships to Eton (1828) and the University of Oxford (1834), but he excelled in sports. He particularly made his mark in rowing and cricket. Though his pursuit of sports was short lived, he claimed that they gave him leadership gifts. "It gave me a power of commanding, managing, organizing and directing, seeing through men's capabilities and using every man in the post to which he was best suited, bearing and forbearing, keeping men around me in good temper, which I have found of infinite use on lots of occasions in life, though in very different matters."

In 1837, before graduation, Ryle contracted a serious chest infection, which caused him to turn to the Bible and prayer for the first time in over fourteen years. One Sunday he entered church late as Ephesians 2:8 was being read – slowly, phrase by phrase. John felt the Lord was speaking to him personally, and he claims to have been converted at that moment through the Word without any commentary or sermon.

His biographer wrote, "He came under conviction, was converted, and from that moment to the last recorded syllable of this life, no doubt ever lingered in John's mind that the Word of God was living and powerful, sharper than any two-edged sword."

After graduation from Oxford, John went to London to study law for his career in politics, but in 1841, his father's bank crashed. That was the end of the career in politics, for he had no funding to continue.

In later years, John wrote, "We got up one summer's morning with all the world before us as usual, and went to bed that same night completely and entirely ruined. The immediate consequences were bitter and painful in the extreme, and humiliating to the utmost degree."

And at another time, he said, "The plain fact was there was no one of the family whom it touched more than it did me. My father and mother were no longer young and in the downhill of life; my brothers and sisters, of course, never expected to live at Henbury (the family home) and naturally never thought of it as their house after a certain time. I, on the contrary, as the eldest son, twenty-five, with all the world before me, lost everything, and saw the whole future of my life turned upside down and thrown into confusion."

After this financial ruin from abundance, Ryle was a commoner – all in a day. For the first time in his life, he needed a job. His education qualified him for the clergy, so with his Oxford degree, he was ordained and entered the ministry of the Church of England. He proceeded in a totally different direction with his first assignment in the ministry at Exbury in Hampshire, but it was a rural area riddled with disease. His recurring lung infection made a difficult couple of years until he was transferred to St. Thomas in Winchester. With his commanding presence, passionately held principles, and warm disposition, John's congregation grew so large and strong it needed different accommodations.

Ryle accepted a position at that time in Helmington, Suffolk, where he had much time to read theologians like Wesley, Bunyan, Knox, Calvin, and Luther. He was a contemporary of Charles Spurgeon, Dwight Moody, George Mueller, and Hudson Taylor. He lived in the age of Dickens, Darwin, and the American Civil War. All of these influenced Ryle's understanding and theology.

His writing career began from the tragedy of the Great Yarmouth suspension bridge. On May 9, 1845, a large crowd gathered for the official grand opening festivities, but the bridge collapsed and more than a hundred people plunged into the water and drowned. The incident shocked the whole country but it led Ryle to write his first tract. He spoke of life's uncertainties and God's sure provision of salvation through Jesus Christ. Thousands of copies were sold.

That same year, he married Matilda Plumptre, but she died after only two years, leaving him with an infant daughter. In 1850, he married Jessie Walker, but she had a lingering sickness, which caused Ryle to care for her and their growing family (three sons and another daughter) for ten years until she died. In 1861, he was transferred to Stradbroke, Suffolk, where he married Henrietta Clowes.

Stradbroke, Suffolk, was Ryle's last parish, and he gained a reputation for his straightforward preaching and evangelism. Besides his travelling and preaching, he spent time writing. He wrote more than 300 pamphlets, tracts, and books. His books include *Expository Thoughts on the Gospels* (7 Volumes, 1856-1869), *Principles for Churchmen* (1884), *Home Truths, Knots Untied, Old Paths,* and *Holiness.*

His *Christian Leaders of the Eighteenth Century* (1869) is described as having "short, pithy sentences, compelling logic and penetrating insight into spiritual power." This seems to be the case with most of his writing as he preached and wrote with five main guidelines: (1) Have a clear view of the subject, (2) Use simple words, (3) Use a simple style of composition, (4) Be direct, and (5) Use plenty of anecdotes and illustrations.

In all of his success with writing, he used the royalties to pay his father's debts. He may have felt indebted to that financial ruin, for he said, "I have not the least doubts, it was all for the best. If I had not been ruined, I should never have been a clergyman, never preached a sermon, or written a tract or book."

In spite of all of the trials that Ryle experienced – financial ruin, loss of three wives, his own poor health – he learned several life lessons. First, care and tend to your own family. Second, swim against the tide when you need to. He was evangelical before it was popular and he held to principles of Scripture: justification by faith alone, substitutionary atonement, the Trinity, and preaching. Third, model Christian attitudes toward your opponents. Fourth, learn and understand church history. Important benefits come from past generations. Fifth, serve in old age; "die in the harness." And, sixth, persevere through your trials.

These were life principles that Ryle learned as he lived his life, as he preached, as he wrote, and as he spread the gospel. He was forever a supporter of evangelism and a critic of ritualism.

J. C. Ryle was recommended by Prime Minister Benjamin Disraeli to be Bishop of Liverpool in 1880 where he then worked to build churches and mission halls to reach the whole city. He retired in 1900 at the age of 83 and died later that year. His successor described him as "a man of granite with a heart of a child."

G. C. B. Davies said "a commanding presence and fearless advocacy of his principles were combined with a kind and understanding attitude in his personal relationships."[1]

---

1   Sources:

William P. Farley, "J. C. Ryle: A 19th-century Evangelical," *Enrichment Journal*, http://enrichmentjournal.ag.org/200604/200604_120_jcryle.cfm.

"J. C. Ryle," *The Banner of Truth*, https://banneroftruth.org/us/about/banner-authors/j-c-ryle/.

"J. C. Ryle," *Theopedia*, https://www.theopedia.com/john-charles-ryle.

David Holloway, "J. C. Ryle – The Man, The Minister and The Missionary," *Bible Bulletin Board*, http://www.biblebb.com/files/ryle/j_c_ryle.htm.

Other Similar Titles

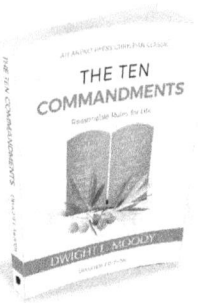

The Ten Commandments,
by Dwight L. Moody

The ten commandments are not popular today. Atheists want them nowhere in sight. Many Christians say they are outdated. But Dwight L. Moody challenges us to take a closer look. Which of the ten commandments can we honestly say are not good? Which of the ten commandments can we break and not suffer the consequences, both here and in eternity?

This book will challenge you to examine God's rules for life. God doesn't ask anything of us that is difficult or unreasonable, and this is certainly true with Jesus Christ as our strength and the Holy Spirit to guide us. This book is a challenging yet refreshing look at some of the oldest, most well-known words of God.

Available where books are sold.

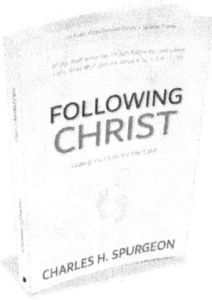

Following Christ,
by Charles H. Spurgeon

You cannot have Christ if you will not serve Him. If you take Christ, you must take Him in all His qualities. You must not simply take Him as a Friend, but you must also take Him as your Master. If you are to become His disciple, you must also become His servant. God-forbid that anyone fights against that truth. It is certainly one of our greatest delights on earth to serve our Lord, and this is to be our joyful vocation even in heaven itself: *His servants shall serve Him: and they shall see His face* (Revelation 22:3-4).

Available where books are sold.

Heaven,
by Dwight L. Moody

The goal of this book is to whet your appetite for heaven. A careful look at Scripture reveals that heaven is what every born-again believer is longing for. Our time on earth is only in a temporary dwelling place, and heaven is the true home of all God's children. A study of heaven can change how you approach each day, and even how you view others around you. As real as this life is, we are assured that heaven is just as real. While we must not neglect our present God-given duties, we must at the same time be preparing for our future home and should even be looking forward with great anticipation to our eternal home.

Available where books are sold.

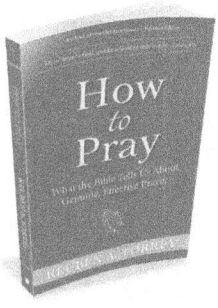

How to Pray,
by Reuben A. Torrey

Great revivals always begin first in the hearts of a few men and women whom God arouses by His Spirit to believe in Him as a living God, as a God who answers prayer, and upon whose heart He lays a burden from which no rest can be found except in persistent crying unto God.

May God use this book to inspire many who are currently prayerless, or nearly so, to pray earnestly. May God stir up your own heart to be one of those burdened to pray, and to pray until God answers.

Available where books are sold.

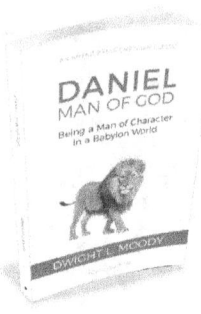

Daniel, Man of God,
by Dwight L. Moody

God will exalt us when the time is right. We needn't try to promote ourselves; we needn't struggle for position. Let God put us where He wants us and let us be true to God. It is better for a man to be right with God, even if he holds no great earthly position. It is honest and humble men whom God will promote, if He so desires.

This study illustrates what Daniel did, and also what Daniel didn't do, which caught the attention of God and kings alike. Few are the men in history of Daniel's caliber, even though the principles he followed can be implemented by all. Are you ready to be a truly great man, one that will cause God and men to take notice?

Available where books are sold.

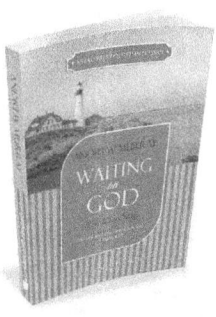

Waiting on God,
by Andrew Murray

Too little time is given to waiting on the Lord at our conventions and assemblies, and in our private devotions. Isn't He willing to make things right in His own divine way? Has the life of God's people reached the utmost limit of what He is willing to do for them? Surely not. We need to wait on Him and put away our experiences, however blessed they have been; our personal concept of truth, however sound and scriptural we think it is; our plans, however needful and suitable they appear. We must give the Lord time and place to show us what He could do and what He will do. The Lord has new developments and new resources. He can do new things, unheard-of things, and hidden things. Let us enlarge our hearts and not limit Him.

Available where books are sold.

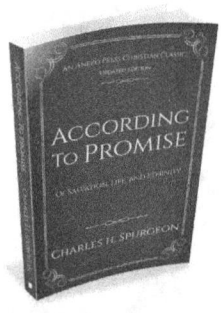

According to Promise,
by Charles H. Spurgeon

The first part of this book is meant to be a sieve to separate the chaff from the wheat. Use it on your own soul. It may be the most profitable and beneficial work you have ever done. He who looked into his accounts and found that his business was losing money was saved from bankruptcy. This may happen also to you. If, however, you discover that your heavenly business is prospering, it will be a great comfort to you. You cannot lose by honestly searching your own heart.

The second part of this book examines God's promises to His children. The promises of God not only exceed all precedent, but they also exceed all imitation. No one has been able to compete with God in the language of liberality. The promises of God are as much above all other promises as the heavens are above the earth.

Available where books are sold.

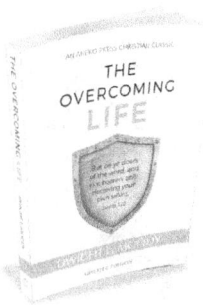

The Overcoming Life,
by Dwight L. Moody

Are you an overcomer? Or, are you plagued by little sins that easily beset you? Even worse, are you failing in your Christian walk, but refuse to admit and address it? No Christian can afford to dismiss the call to be an overcomer. The earthly cost is minor; the eternal reward is beyond measure.

Dwight L. Moody uses stories and humor to bring to light the essential principles of successful Christian living. Each aspect of overcoming is looked at from a practical and understandable angle. The solution Moody presents for our problems is not religion, rules, or other outward corrections. Instead, he takes us to the heart of the matter and prescribes biblical, God-given remedies for every Christian's life. Get ready to embrace genuine victory for today, and joy for eternity.

Available where books are sold.

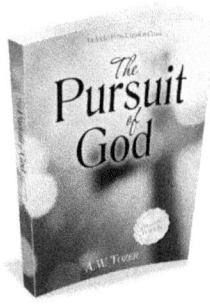

The Pursuit of God,
by A. W. Tozer

To have found God and still to pursue Him is a paradox of love, scorned indeed by the too-easily-satisfied religious person, but justified in happy experience by the children of the burning heart. Saint Bernard of Clairvaux stated this holy paradox in a musical four-line poem that will be instantly understood by every worshipping soul:

We taste Thee, O Thou Living Bread,
And long to feast upon Thee still:
We drink of Thee, the Fountainhead
And thirst our souls from Thee to fill.

Come near to the holy men and women of the past and you will soon feel the heat of their desire after God. Let A. W. Tozer's pursuit of God spur you also into a genuine hunger and thirst to truly know God.

Available where books are sold.

Pilgrim's Progress,
by John Bunyan

Often disguised as something that would help him, evil accompanies Christian on his journey to the Celestial City. As you walk with him, you'll begin to identify today's many religious pitfalls. These are presented by men such as Pliable, who turns back at the Slough of Despond; and Ignorance, who believes he's a true follower of Christ when he's really only trusting in himself. Each character represented in this allegory is intentionally and profoundly accurate in its depiction of what we see all around us, and unfortunately, what we too often see in ourselves. But while Christian is injured and nearly killed, he eventually prevails to the end. So can you.

Available where books are sold.

www.ingramcontent.com/pod-product-compliance
Lightning Source LLC
Chambersburg PA
CBHW070152080526
44586CB00015B/1955